Made in the USA
Monee, IL
15 March 2021

62796023R00111